THE STORY OF CHRISTMAS

Retold by Anita Ganeri

DORLING KINDERSLEY

London • New York • Stuttgart

"A town in Galilee, named Nazareth"

Long ago, in the town of Nazareth in Galilee, lived a girl called Mary. She lived with her family in a small house on the edge of the town. Mary often helped her mother with the household chores. She sang as she worked and chatted to friends who came to visit.

Mary was engaged to be married to a man called Joseph. He was a good man, who worked as a carpenter in Nazareth.

"Fear not Mary, thou hast found favour with God"

One day, when Mary was busy baking bread, a shining figure suddenly appeared before her.

Mary was alarmed and dropped the bread in fright. This was the angel Gabriel. He had come to deliver a special message from God.

"Don't be afraid Mary. God has chosen you to be the mother of a baby."

"You shall call him Jesus. He will be a very special king."

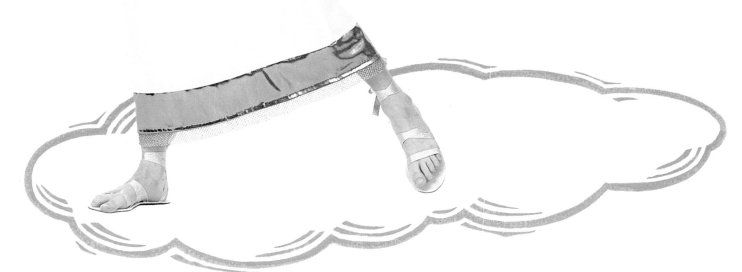

Mary hurried to tell Joseph the news. He was troubled and wondered if he should still marry Mary now that she was expecting a baby.

But that night, in a dream, an angel told Joseph to go ahead with the marriage – all would be well.

"Unto the city of David, called Bethlehem"

Soon after Mary and Joseph were married, the emperor gave an order. Everyone had to go to the town where they were born to be counted.

Joseph had been born in Bethlehem, far away. So Mary and Joseph packed up their belongings and set off on the journey.

Days later, they reached Bethlehem, dusty and tired. The town was crowded with people.

"There was no room for them at the inn"

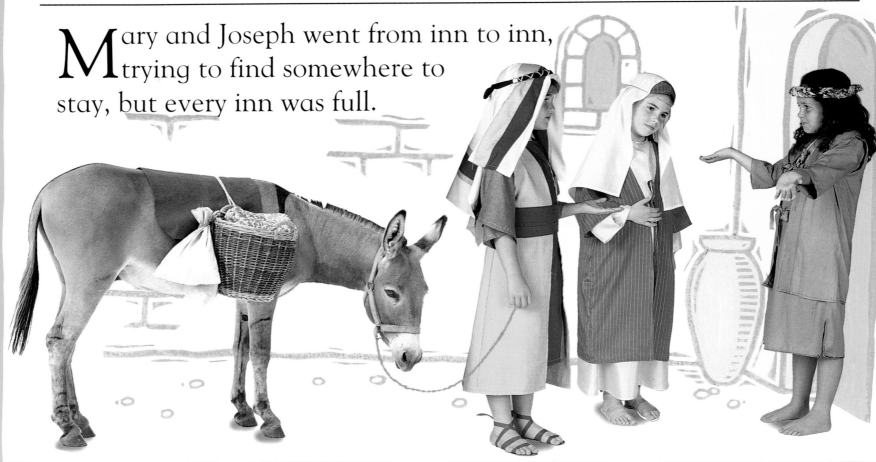

Mary and Joseph went from inn to inn, trying to find somewhere to stay, but every inn was full.

Finally, a kind innkeeper took pity on them. He had no spare rooms, but he did have a stable.

Mary was worried. She knew that her baby could be born at any time now.

Mary peered inside. The stable looked warm and clean. The couple were happy to find a place to rest at last.

"And the time came for the baby to be born"

Later that night, in the snug little stable, Mary's son was born.

She called him Jesus, the name the angel had given her, and wrapped him warmly in a blanket.

Gently, Mary laid
Jesus in a manger,
filled with soft hay.

Mary and Joseph
smiled happily at
each other. They knew
Jesus was a very special baby.

Later, Mary rested while
Joseph watched over
her and the baby.
"How peaceful they look,"
he thought tenderly.

"There were shepherds abiding in the fields"

Meanwhile, on a nearby hillside, some shepherds were watching over their sheep. They gathered together to tell each other stories through the night.

Suddenly, a brilliant, shining light filled the sky and an angel appeared before the fearful shepherds.

"I bring you good tidings of great joy."

"This day, a baby has been born in Bethlehem. You will find him lying in a manger."

17

"Glory to God in the highest"

As the shepherds looked up, astonished, the sky became ablaze with light. Angels appeared, shining brighter than the brightest stars, singing and praising God.

"Peace on Earth."

"Goodwill to all people."

Then, just as suddenly, the angels were gone. The shepherds were very excited.

"We must go to Bethlehem at once, to see the baby and worship him."

And off they went, taking a tiny lamb with them as a gift.

"They found the baby lying in a manger"

The shepherds hurried to Bethlehem as fast as they could go. There, in the stable, they found Mary, Joseph, and the baby Jesus.

The shepherds knelt quietly by the manger, careful not to wake the sleeping baby. They gave the lamb to Mary as a gift for the baby Jesus, then returned to their sheep in the hills.

On the way back, they told everyone they met about the amazing things they had seen and heard.

"For we have seen his star in the east"

Far away in the east, some wise men saw a bright new star in the sky. The star was a sign that a king had been born.

The wise men followed the star to Jerusalem, in search of the new ruler.

King Herod was furious when he heard about the new king. He summoned the wise men to him and demanded that they return to him, once they had found the baby.

Herod pretended he wanted to worship the new king, but really he wanted to kill him.

So the wise men left Jerusalem and continued on their journey across the desert.

23

"Lo, the star went before them"

It guided them on their way, leading them to the town of Bethlehem.

The wise men rested by day and travelled by night so that they could follow the great star.

Once the star had reached Bethlehem, it shone even brighter than before. Finally, it came to rest over the place where Jesus lay.

They had found the king at last!

"They presented unto him gifts"

The wise men went into the stable, carrying gifts for Jesus. They brought caskets of precious gold, sweet-smelling frankincense, and healing myrrh.

The wise men bowed down
and worshipped the baby.
 Later that night, each
was warned in a dream not
to return to King Herod. So
they went back to their
country by a different route.

27

"Take the child and flee to Egypt"

Soon after, Joseph was warned in a dream of King Herod's wicked plan to kill Jesus. An angel told him to escape to Egypt with his family.

Joseph woke Mary. Quietly, they gathered up their belongings and crept away through the narrow streets of Bethlehem.

Their journey took many days, but finally, they reached Egypt safely.

Here they stayed until an angel brought Joseph good news – King Herod was dead! Now it was safe for them to return home.

Each year, we celebrate the birth of the baby Jesus. We call this special time "Christmas".

29